P9-CEK-111

Merry Christmas 1992
from aunt Ruth

A Touch of His Wisdom

Other Books in This Series

A Touch of His Wisdom

MEDITATIONS ON THE BOOK OF PROVERBS WITH ORIGINAL PHOTOGRAPHS BY

CHARLES STANLEY

ZondervanPublishingHouse

Grand Rapids, Michigan

A Division of HarperCollinsPublishers

A Touch of His Wisdom
Copyright © 1992 by Charles Stanley

Requests for information should be addressed to:
Zondervan Publishing House
Grand Rapids, Michigan 49530

Library of Congress Cataloging-in-Publication Data

Stanley, Charles F.
    A touch of his wisdom : meditations on the book of Proverbs /
Charles Stanley.
        p.   cm.
    ISBN 0-310-54540-4
    1. Bible. O.T. Proverbs—Meditations. I. Title.
    BS1465.4.S73   1992
    242'.5—dc20   91–46476
                                                                        CIP

The author wishes to express his appreciation to Tim Olive for his technical
assistance with the photographs and to Jim Daily for his editorial assistance.

All Scripture quotations, unless otherwise noted, are taken from the HOLY
BIBLE: NEW INTERNATIONAL VERSION® (North American Edition).
Copyright © 1973, 1978, 1984, by the International Bible Society. Used by
permission of Zondervan Publishing House.

"NIV" and "New International Version" are registered in the United States
Patent and Trademark Office by the International Bible Society.

All rights reserved. No part of this publication may be reproduced, stored in a
retrieval system, or transmitted in any form or by any means—electronic,
mechanical, photocopy, recording, or any other—except for brief quotations in
printed reviews, without the prior permission of the publisher.

Edited by Gerard Terpstra
Cover design, interior design, and line illustrations by Art Jacobs

Printed in the United States of America

92 93 94 95 96 / AK / 9 8 7 6 5 4 3 2 1

This edition is printed on acid-free paper and meets the American National
Standards Institute Z39.48 standard.

Contents

Photographs

Introduction

*W*hen I am faced with difficult decisions or challenges, I ask myself this question: "What is the wise thing to do?"

I am amazed at how often I turn to the book of Proverbs, where I discover so many of God's principles for wise living and decision making.

A Touch of His Wisdom is a collection of verses from each of the thirty-one chapters of Proverbs that have personally helped me to know and understand God's ways.

Wisdom is gaining God's perspective on life and applying it to particular circumstances. Proverbs clearly reveals his divine perspective on many of today's most pressing issues—morality, marriage, parenting, work, relationships, and finances, to name a few.

When I seek and apply God's wisdom, I can experience God's success rather than my failure. His order and peace replace my confusion, and I learn to lean on his faithfulness instead of succumbing to my fears or worries.

I am so glad that God is not reluctant to share his counsel with us. In fact, he says that if we lack wisdom, we can confidently ask for his insight and he will provide his timely answer (James 1:5–6).

It is my prayer that each of these chapters in *A Touch of His Wisdom* will reveal some facet of God's character and ways to help you in your daily Christian walk.

I pray along with the apostle Paul that God will "fill you with the knowledge of his will through all spiritual wisdom and understanding" (Col. 1:9).

The wise man or woman will bring honor to God through biblically sound decisions and will experience the priceless blessings of obedience to God.

Nothing can compare to knowing and obeying the wisdom of God. It is "more profitable than silver and yields better returns than gold" (Prov. 3:14).

A Touch of His Wisdom

The fear of the Lord is the beginning of knowledge.
Proverbs 1:7

The Foundation of Wisdom

*W*isdom is knowing and doing what is right. Not simply knowing, but making the right use of that knowledge. One may possess a vast storehouse of knowledge but still be unwise. True wisdom begins with a knowledge of and reverence for God as revealed through his Son Jesus Christ. This is the foundation on which to build a life that can courageously withstand the inevitable storms of criticism, pain, loss, temptation, and success.

The Scriptures are God's wisdom. They teach us who God is and reveal how he acts and thinks. They instruct us to distinguish right from wrong, and they give clear guidelines for practical living. His Word is counsel from heaven for life on earth, revealing the Father's omniscient heart to help us walk victoriously in all of our endeavors.

When learned and consistently applied, God's Word fastens firmly together the disjointed portions of our lives—our work, our family, our relationships, our dreams, our thoughts, our words, our deeds—in the sturdy framework of divine wisdom.

The starting point for distilling God's wisdom for everyday life is a profound reverence and honor for him. The "fear of the LORD" implies a sincere hatred and repentance of every sin (Prov. 8:13), combined with genuine, growing awe of his character, attributes, and personhood. (Ex. 15:11) One who fears God shuns evil and seeks good, cultivating his soul for the planting of God's Word.

We cannot know and honor God without first acknowledging our sin, receiving Christ's forgiveness, and establishing a new relationship with the Father through faith in Christ's work on the cross. Our knowledge grows as we depend on the power of the

Holy Spirit to impart to us the mind of Christ for every circumstance.

Each day can bring a new appreciation of the wonderful character and attributes of God—his holiness, righteousness, mercy, grace, love, and comfort. The more we worship, adore, and obey him, the more we experience the blessings of his wisdom.

A sincere reverence for God is the supernatural tool that embeds the Scriptures into the depths of our hearts, penetrating our innermost being with the ageless and perfect wisdom of the Carpenter from Nazareth.

The fear of the Lord is the foundation of a life built with wisdom. It is the first step toward a new adventure in knowing and following Jesus Christ.

Lord, I am grateful for who you are and what you have done for me. I need your wisdom every day. Bring together the pieces of my life with a new appreciation for your Word and a fresh commitment to obedience. I know that fearing you does not mean I am afraid of you but that I respect and revere your majestic name. You have promised that you will give me the discernment and insight I need as I grow in my reverence for you. I am excited about building my life on the wisdom of your Word.

TOUCHSTONE

The life built on the wisdom of God endures forever.

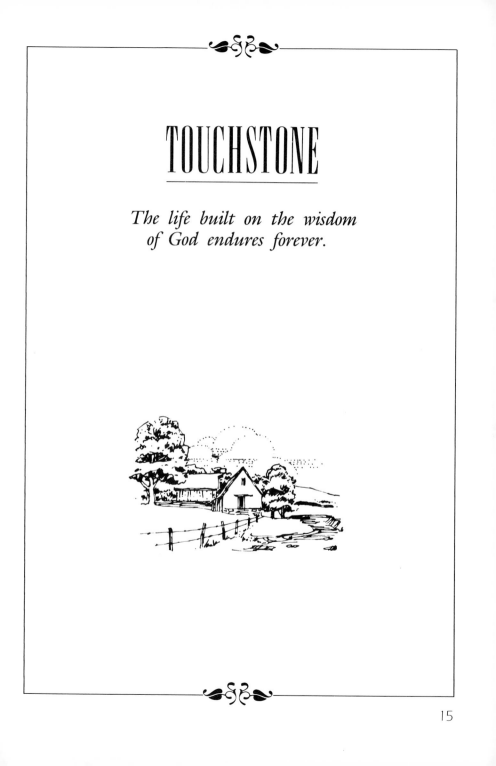

Wisdom will enter your heart,
and knowledge will be pleasant to your soul.

Proverbs 2:10

Ask and Seek

*G*od wants us to be wise. We, too, yearn for more wisdom and understanding. But how do we receive and grow in discernment and knowledge?

We recognize God as the source of all wisdom: "For the LORD gives wisdom, and from his mouth come knowledge and understanding" (Prov. 2:6).

If added together, all of the educational institutions in the world, all the books in all the libraries of every nation, and all the minds of the most astute intellectuals in every profession would be but a millimeter of intelligence compared to the fathomless mind of omniscient God—Creator, Sustainer, and End of all creation. Once we know him through faith in Christ, his flawless wisdom is accessible to counsel, guide, correct, and enlighten us in every circumstance, every problem, every need.

All we need to do to avail ourselves of his wisdom is ask. "If any of you lacks wisdom, he should ask God, who gives generously to all without finding fault, and it will be given to him" (James 1:5).

That almost seems too simple, doesn't it? We must remember, however, that we can know God and his ways only when he chooses to reveal himself and enlighten us through his Word and his Spirit. It is a matter of grace, and asking is the doorway to receiving the fullness of his grace.

Notice how abundantly and lavishly God gives. He does not begrudge us his wisdom according to our past behavior. He realizes our frailty and total dependence on him for fruitfulness, consistency, and maturity. His hand is overflowing with loving-kindness, extended without measure or limit.

When his father David died, Solomon became Israel's king. Although Solomon had the extraordinary education and amenities of a ruler's son, he knew he lacked the wisdom necessary to govern the nation of Israel.

One night the Lord appeared to Solomon in a dream and

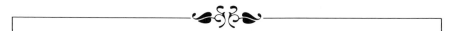

made this astounding offer: "Ask for whatever you want me to give you" (1 Kings 3:5). Solomon's response was prompt: "Give your servant a discerning heart to govern your people and to distinguish between right and wrong" (v. 9).

Is that the cry of your heart? Would you rather gain riches, power, status, or beauty—or wisdom from God?

If you want wisdom, look to God only. Ask for it confidently. Eagerly anticipate his response. He is just as willing to impart his wisdom to you as he did to Solomon.

Wisdom should be our chief desire, and it *is* for the asking.

God, how desperately I need your wisdom and how grateful I am that you are the only wise God. Thank you that you liberally share your truth. I ask you for your wisdom and expect that I will have precisely the insight and information I need to do your will. Thank you for forgiving me my sins so that I can receive your wisdom by faith and grace. I have made many mistakes, but I hope to make far fewer as I learn more about you and apply your wisdom to my daily tasks.

TOUCHSTONE

Wisdom is for the asking.

Trust in the Lord with all your heart
and lean not on your own understanding;
in all your ways acknowledge him,
and he will make your paths straight.

Proverbs 3:5–6

Trust and Obey

When I was a teenager Proverbs 3:5–6 became my spiritual compass. Whenever I faced a difficult decision, I always turned to it for assurance. God etched its simple but profound truth in my mind and heart. It continues to be a signpost along life's road, ever pointing me to the bottom line for all decisions: trust and obey God. It is an eternal combination that always makes one a winner.

Why? Because God is trustworthy. He is dependable. He is sovereignly working everything together for his glory and our good.

His wisdom is given to those who look to him, lean on him, rely on him. The more we depend on our Father for instruction, strength, hope, and guidance, the more abundantly he confers on us his divine wisdom.

We cannot receive wisdom from God apart from a relationship with him. God is not interested in teaching his ways to those who have no desire to please him or follow him. He does yearn, however, to teach men and women who are bold enough to believe his promises and carry out his commands.

Trusting in the Lord means that we place our present and future circumstances in his hands, confident in his ability to orchestrate people and events to achieve his will. This whole-hearted trust brings a secure peace of mind and contentment. Putting our full emotional and volitional weight on the faithfulness of God activates his promises.

There is one catch, however. We must first admit our inadequacy: "Lean not on your own understanding." That was Solomon's attitude when he confessed, "But I am only a little child and do not know how to carry out my duties" (1 Kings 3:7).

This is where many Christians falter. We can do many things quite well without any apparent need for God's wisdom. We can repair items, invent machines, program computers, hike trails, and perform multitudes of other activities with very little sense of God's participation.

Yet we have been created by God to work in a world he fashioned with his own hands. Our lives, our very breath, is in his hands; our minds and bodies are his gifts. His wisdom is displayed in everything, even when we fail to recognize him.

God has given you talents and skills. However, they are maximized for eternity when you trust him to direct and use them for his plans. The question is, Will you lean on your own understanding or depend on God?

The wise choice is obvious when we understand that God knows the end from the beginning and sustains all things in between. Trusting him is the wisest decision we can make. Depending on our frail discernment limits us to a narrow, finite existence, restricted by circumstances and experiences we cannot control. Relying on God's wisdom adds a supernatural dimension that cannot be matched by anything on earth.

Father, keep me ever mindful of my inadequacy and your sufficiency. Continue to assure me that to lean on you is not a sign of weakness but of wisdom. I want always to remember that to obey you is not only right but always the wise choice— the decision that never fails to bring the richest rewards.

TOUCHSTONE

*Trusting God is the wisest
decision you can make.*

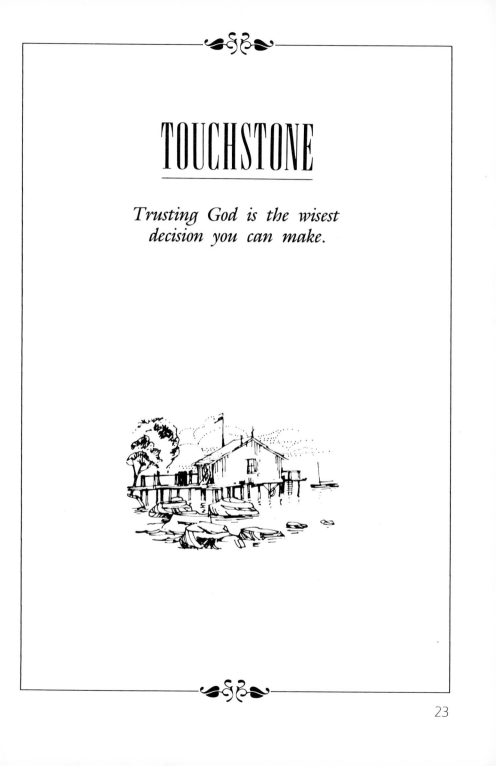

Above all else, guard your heart,
for it is the wellspring of life.

Proverbs 4:23

The Wellspring
of Life

A small village heard about an enemy's plan to poison their water supply. Although several small streams flowed through the village, the leaders stationed their security force at one location—the lone pool from where the springs flowed. Their tactic worked perfectly. The security force seized the saboteurs at dusk as they approached the pool.

Satan has a similar strategy. He launches his most damaging assaults at the one area that most influences our behavior—the heart. In the vocabulary of the Bible, the heart represents the center of personality, soul, mind, will, and emotion.

The heart is the command and control system for our lives. As God's wisdom is received and cultivated through the inner working of the Holy Spirit, our lives reflect the presence and influence of Jesus Christ. But to the extent that we neglect or ignore the wellspring of the heart, our actions can become polluted by our adversary, the Devil, damaging our relationships, destroying our joy, and diluting our testimony.

We guard our hearts from sin's bitter defilement by treasuring God's Word in our hearts (Ps. 119:9–11). The more we study, meditate on, and practice the precepts of God, the safer the inner sanctuary of our heart will be. God's Word cleanses us, corrects us, exhorts us, encourages us, straining out impure motivations and planting the seed of the Scriptures in our innermost being.

We can also protect the wellspring of our soul by the consistent exercise of prayer. Jesus instructed his disciples to "watch and pray" so that they would not "fall into temptation" (Matt. 26:41). Prayer is conscious fellowship with and dependence on Jesus Christ. When we pray with zeal and humility, recognizing our frailty and God's power, we are alerted to the

Devil's deception and will turn quickly to the Father for his unfailing help.

Healthy, periodic self-examination is also a safeguard. Directed by the Holy Spirit, we ask God to search us and sift out any willful sin or camouflaged area of disobedience. "Watch your life and doctrine closely," Paul reminded Timothy (1 Tim. 4:16); and it is good advice for us as well. As the Spirit of God convicts us of sin or reveals an area of subtle rebellion, we repent and receive a fresh anointing and protection from God.

The issues of life, the essential matters, flow from the heart, determining the direction and impact of our lives. Guard your heart earnestly; and the wellspring of the Holy Spirit will overflow into all you do, say, and think.

Dear Father, I want you to establish your truth in my innermost being. I am sometimes so easily distracted and disturbed by outward circumstances that I neglect to cultivate a genuine devotion to you. Work through your Spirit to remove any false way and teach me to guard my heart through your indwelling presence. Control my thoughts and motivations and bring me into conformity with your will.

TOUCHSTONE

*Guard your heart, and you
will guard your life.*

For a man's ways are in full view of the Lord,
and he examines all his paths.

Proverbs 5:21

Our God Who Really Sees

W hen Hagar was cast out of Abraham's camp because of Sarah's jealousy over her pregnancy, Hagar found herself abandoned on the roadside. There God met her with grace and love, promising her his help.

Grateful, she exclaimed, "You are the God who sees me" (Gen. 16:13). She ascribed a new name to God—El Roi, meaning "the God who really sees."

Our all-knowing, all-wise God is also our all-seeing God. His presence permeates all we do. We live and move and have our being in him. We walk before him each day, our hearts opened before him. He sees our pain, our discouragement, our confusion, our heartache, our struggles. And in the seeing, he comes to our rescue with amazing grace.

Understanding that every detail of our lives is laid bare before our heavenly Father and that we are in his all-sufficient care should move us to profound awe and adoration. We exclaim with David: "O LORD, you have searched me and you know me. You know when I sit and when I rise; you perceive my thoughts from afar. You discern my going out and my lying down; you are familiar with all my ways. Before a word is on my tongue you know it completely, O LORD. . . . Such knowledge is too wonderful for me, too lofty for me to attain" (Ps. 139:1–4, 6).

God sees your life from beginning to end. He numbered your days and ordered your steps while you were yet in your mother's womb. Seeing your plight brought about by sin, he sent his Son to save you from death and eternal destruction.

God's comprehensive knowledge of our ways should likewise encourage us to live obediently and honestly before him. It is futile for you to attempt to conceal your true feelings and actions. Even when you sin, you do so in the presence of God.

There is not one act, one thought, one ambition, one indiscretion that is hidden from his sight. "Nothing in all creation is hidden from God's sight. Everything is uncovered and laid bare before the eyes of him to whom we must give account" (Heb. 4:13).

Even our inner secrets are exposed to the penetrating gaze of God. Rather than frighten us, this should cause us to seek to please our Father, who treats us not according to our deeds but according to his mercy and grace in Jesus Christ.

We should be transparent in our relationship with him, realizing that even our foulest sins cannot separate us from his unfailing love. Our relationships with others should also be grounded on integrity and sincerity, as we attempt to avoid every form of hypocrisy.

The God who sees is the One who watches over us from before birth through death. He is with us and for us in all things, never condemning but always loving us.

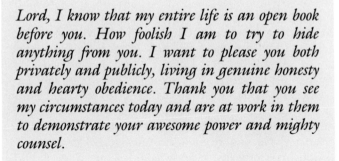

Lord, I know that my entire life is an open book before you. How foolish I am to try to hide anything from you. I want to please you both privately and publicly, living in genuine honesty and hearty obedience. Thank you that you see my circumstances today and are at work in them to demonstrate your awesome power and mighty counsel.

TOUCHSTONE

*Nothing can separate you
from God's perfect love.*

Can a man scoop fire into his lap
without his clothes being burned?
Can a man walk on hot coals
without his feet being scorched?

Proverbs 6:27−28

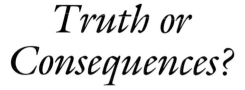

Truth or Consequences?

*W*isdom is the godly pathway to success, activating the blessings of God when we do his work in his way.

Decisions based on the faultless principles of the Scriptures will stand the test of time and criticism. Behavior motivated by loving obedience to God's commands will produce character that is solid and enduring, unaffected by the whims of circumstance and changing morality.

As surely as obedience to God's wisdom begets blessings, disobedience and rebellion ensure eventual chaos and disarray. When the Bible says the "wages of sin is death" (Rom. 6:23), it not only states sin's devastating penalty but also illustrates a divinely decreed principle: Sin always brings negative consequences.

We cannot act contrary to God's revealed truth and expect his favor and help. The apostle Paul put it this way: "Do not be deceived: God cannot be mocked. A man reaps what he sows" (Gal. 6:7).

Foolishness, the antithesis of biblical wisdom, will cause us to reap what we sow, more than we sow, later than we sow. Failure to comply with the truth of God's Word is thus a very serious and somber matter.

Each act of sin is a seed of insubordination to God's authority, planted in the soil of rebellion, bringing a bitter harvest. We cannot get away with sin. We cannot neglect the wisdom of God and expect to enjoy his blessings.

Even if we seemingly manage to avoid the consequences of disobedience, we will one day give an account of our actions before the Judge of all mankind. Justice will be righteously applied, resulting in the loss of reward for the believer and the loss of eternal relationship with God for the unbeliever.

God uses consequences to teach us the value of wisdom. We learn from the outcome of our mistakes that obeying God is far more pleasant and rewarding than neglecting or abusing his truth. Planting seeds of wisdom may be difficult at first, but the harvest is worth the effort.

The wise person lives in accord with God's Word because he knows the immeasurable riches of God's blessings. The foolish person's disobedience is compounded by the harsh and bitter consequences of his actions.

Do not get burned by the consequences of sin. Be wise and enjoy the blessings of submission to the Father's will.

Lord, I choose to be wise by obeying you. Nothing can compare to your blessings that come when I follow you. I know the danger of sin's consequences. Thank you for your grace to help me start anew each morning and for your Spirit to enable me to make the right choices.

TOUCHSTONE

*Before you sow, think of the
harvest you will reap.*

All at once he followed her
like an ox going to the slaughter,
like a deer stepping into a noose.

Proverbs 7:22

Run the Race

When soldiers go into battle, they must be very careful to tread only on ground that has been freed from land mines. A misplaced step into uncleared territory could be deadly.

Our cunning foe, the Devil, operates in similar fashion—concealing and camouflaging his real intentions by setting harmful snares of temptation and deceit. Human wisdom is no match in dealing with his cleverness and craftiness.

The best means to avoid his shrewd traps is to stay on the path of righteousness, walking straight forward in the will and ways of God.

The author of Hebrews termed this "the race marked out for us" (Heb. 12:1). The more we lean on Christ and the course he has marked out for us, the less likely we are to fall into Satan's traps.

But how do we keep on course? The author of Hebrews again provides the key: "Let us fix our eyes on Jesus, the author and perfecter of our faith" (Heb. 12:2).

Like a runner fixing his gaze on the finish line, the believer is to look away from all else that distracts from his personal relationship with Jesus Christ. There are many enticements along the way. Materialism. Success. Sensuality. The more attention we give to them, the more attractive their appeal becomes. To give in, however, is to give allegiance to someone or something other than the lordship of Christ.

The most effective defense is a steadfast gaze of the heart on the majesty and splendor of Jesus Christ. When we discover who he really is—and then dwell on his attributes of mercy, grace, love, holiness, and goodness and concentrate on his true nature—all else pales in comparison.

Keeping Jesus before us means spending daily time in his Word, maintaining a fresh and passionate prayer life, and consistently obeying the principles and truths we learn. Most important, it involves resolute faith in Christ and his promises.

The psalmist wrote about the person who loves the LORD: "His heart is steadfast, trusting in the Lord. His heart is secure, he will have no fear" (Ps. 112:7–8).

Jesus is faithful. He begins and completes your personal walk of faith as you rely on him. There is no temptation that he cannot overcome for you and with you. There is no evil that he cannot deliver you from. There is no obstacle that he cannot overcome on your behalf.

God never fails you. He will keep you from the Evil One by keeping you on the path of righteousness—for his name's sake, by his own power, for his own glory.

Just look to him.

I realize, Lord, that I cannot detect or avoid Satan's subtle snares in my own strength. I need you to help me "run the race" you have charted for my life. Equip me and guide me so that I may not be detoured or distracted from your will. Thank you for making me stand upright again after I do fall.

TOUCHSTONE

*Keep your eyes on Jesus and
off your circumstances.*

Choose my instruction instead of silver,
knowledge rather than choice gold.

Proverbs 8:10

Going Against the Flow

G od's wisdom must be deliberately chosen. We never drift into wisdom. We must make a conscious decision to seek and receive God's divine counsel and instruction: "We must pay more careful attention, therefore, to what we have heard, so that we do not drift away" (Heb. 2:1).

The Mississippi River flows several hundred miles through the heartland of America, surging to its end in southern Louisiana, spilling its last breath into the Gulf of Mexico. For almost its entire length, its banks are littered with debris and driftwood that became caught up in its enormous torrent and were tossed aside along its meandering journey.

Unless we make a definite choice to pursue wisdom, we, too, can become swept up in the appealing currents of our age. There are swift tides of human pleasure and attraction that can captivate any believer who is not fully committed to Jesus as Savior, Lord, and Life.

His ways and thoughts are not ours (Isa. 55:8). We should think and act contrary to the world's stream of thought. God says you give to receive; the world says hoard all you can. God says you succeed by serving; the world defines success as upward mobility. God says you are to love your enemies; the world tells you to seek revenge.

Choosing God's wisdom begins with realizing its value: "For wisdom is more precious than rubies, and nothing you desire can compare with her" (Prov. 8:11). The wisdom of God is priceless, without peer. Its worth cannot be calculated. All the riches of the universe are like a beggar's hand when compared to the worth of God's wisdom.

Once we perceive the value of God's wisdom, we realize its unlimited application. It touches all of life, imparting his

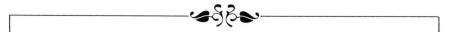

supernatural perspective to all we do and say. His wisdom works anywhere, anytime, in any situation. Its yield of peace, commitment, joy, and blessing is far superior to money, possessions, or status.

Our task is to listen and obey: "Blessed is the man who listens to me, watching daily at my doors, waiting at my doorway" (Prov. 8:34).

Choose God's wisdom. Refuse to be ensnared by the world's deceptions. Dare to trust in the instruction of Christ, diligently cultivating and earnestly appropriating the counsel of God.

Pay close attention to what the Father says. Esteem him above all else, and your life will bear the unmistakable and inestimable fruit of godly wisdom.

Living against the world's flow is difficult, Lord. I want your wisdom, but sometimes I seem to be caught up in so many of this culture's currents. I choose today to seek and pursue your ways. I make this decision in prayerful dependence on you to impart your wisdom to me and teach me your ways. I choose to listen to you daily so I may enjoy the benefits of godly wisdom.

TOUCHSTONE

We never drift into wisdom.

Instruct a wise man and he will be wiser still;
teach a righteous man and he will add to his learning.

Proverbs 9:9

The Classroom of Wisdom

S chool is never out for true saints. They long with unceasing fervor to learn of and know Christ more intimately—the Christ in whom are hidden all the treasures of wisdom and knowledge.

Wisdom cannot be reduced to a formula. It is a right relationship with Christ that provides a biblical context so that we can make wise decisions for every phase of living. However, there is a sacred principle that constitutes an eternal equation for receiving and applying God's wisdom: The degree of wisdom we possess from God is directly proportional to our spirit of humility.

A wise person is not a proud one. Pride and vanity are like poison to the spirit of wisdom. Whoever thinks he is wise is disqualified from God's classroom, where wisdom is given to the contrite of spirit and humble of heart.

Christianity is a growing experience, a deepening relationship with the Savior. You are always in a learning mode as a disciple—literally, a learner—of Jesus Christ. The apostle Paul exemplified the spirit of wisdom when he said, "Not that I have already obtained all this, or have already been made perfect, but I press on to take hold of that for which Christ Jesus took hold of me" (Phil. 3:12).

As believers we must never spend time on the plateau of past accomplishments or present achievements. We must realize we can never plumb the depths of God's wisdom, never exhaust his boundless supply. We should constantly press on to know God (Hos. 6:3), always learning, always seated at the feet of the Master, always awed by the glory and grace of God.

The wise learner understands he is totally dependent on God to reveal his truth. One cannot come to know and fellowship

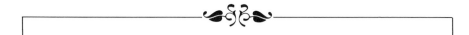

intimately with Christ apart from the benevolent ministry of the Holy Spirit who guides, corrects, instructs, and exhorts. The wise learner is careful to give credit to God alone and not to "venture to speak of anything except what Christ has accomplished through [him]" (Rom. 15:18).

The disciple of Christ learns and matures through Christ's discipline and chastisement. He does not pout or sulk when reproved but understands that the path of godly wisdom is his complete acceptance of God's correction and forgiveness for all his mistakes. Failures are not dead ends but valuable lessons to distill truth from error.

Are you a learner? Do you hunger and thirst for righteousness? Or have you settled for a mediocre life, satisfied with a nominal knowledge of Christ? Wisdom is imparted to the eager student, the meek spirit, the probing mind, the open heart, the repentant soul. Such a person prays, "Show me your ways, O LORD, teach me your paths" (Ps. 25:4).

Are you willing to come to Christ and learn of him?

Father, I realize I am a student in your divine classroom. Place within my heart a thirst to know you and your ways. Then I shall be wise.

TOUCHSTONE

Don't be a dropout in the school of wisdom.

When words are many, sin is not absent,
but he who holds his tongue is wise.

Proverbs 10:19

Tongue Twisters

*D*uring the Second World War, the government of Great Britain was concerned about the infiltration of enemy spies and the security risks they posed. To minimize the danger, government officials placed large posters throughout the nation with this admonition: *Careless talk costs lives.*

Proper use of the tongue is the fruit of wisdom. Careless talk—gossip, innuendo, slander, criticism—hurts people, severs personal relationships, generates hostility and bitterness, and creates discord that can influence generations.

James referred to the tongue as an instrument that charts the course of our lives, making our way smooth or rough, depending on its use. It is a spiritual and emotional rudder, steering us either into conflict or into blessing (James 3:3–8).

When it is used as an instrument of righteousness, in keeping with God's intentions, the tongue is a "fountain of life" (Prov. 10:11), refreshing the discouraged soul. It is as "choice silver" (v. 20), a priceless possession for peaceful, contented living. "The lips of the righteous nourish many" (v. 21), instructing others with the solid truth of God's Word. "The mouth of the righteous brings forth wisdom" (v. 31), giving practical, sound counsel and knows "what is fitting" (v. 32), giving the right answer at the right time.

The wise man's tongue heals, teaches, blesses, encourages, comforts, and promotes godliness. Isn't that what we all desire but find so difficult to achieve?

Speaking words of wisdom begins with a profound transformation of thinking. A person speaks from the treasure of his heart. Our words are but the public pronouncement of the private place of the heart. David said, "May the words of my mouth and the meditation of my heart be pleasing in your sight, O LORD, my Rock and my Redeemer" (Ps. 19:14).

Ask the Holy Spirit to produce in you the fruit of godly speech by working the soil of your heart with his kindness and

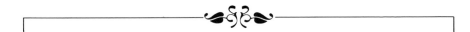

goodness. Esteem others more important than yourself and realize that when you speak disparagingly of another, you are belittling God's special and beloved creation.

Resolve not to speak evil of a person who is not in your presence. Most unruly speech is found in discussions about a third person where only two are gathered. Allow God to tame your speech by quieting the tongue. "When words are many, sin is not absent, but he who holds his tongue is wise" (Prov. 10:19). Refrain from the urge to always express your opinion.

God can use your speech to praise him and edify others, leaving behind a harvest of righteousness that bears fruit in the lives of many people. Allow God to guard your lips by sifting what flows into your mind and filtering what flows out through the purity of his Holy Spirit. You will be amazed at the difference a wise tongue can make.

I must admit, Lord, I have great trouble controlling my tongue. In fact, I can't. Unless you work in my heart to transform my thinking, my words will reveal the ugliness of sin. Cleanse me from my unrighteousness. Show me how to reduce my volume of words while you cleanse me and implant your wisdom in my heart. I want to bless others with my tongue, not hurt them. Make my mouth an instrument of righteousness through the power of the Holy Spirit, who resides at the fountainhead of my speech—my heart.

TOUCHSTONE

*Control your tongue, or your
tongue will control you.*

*A generous man will prosper;
and he who refreshes others
will himself be refreshed.*

Proverbs 11:25

Give, and
It Won't Hurt

*T*he apostle Paul said that the sum of wisdom, the height and depth and breadth of its infinite storehouse, is found in Christ "in whom are hidden all the treasures of wisdom and knowledge" (Col. 2:3).

However, Jesus does not hoard his wisdom. Rather, he gives without measure. He gives his grace abundantly. He gives his guidance freely. He gives his comfort lovingly. The ultimate expression of giving came on the cross where he willingly sacrificed himself for man: "He who did not spare his own Son, but gave him up for us all—how will he not also, along with him, graciously give us all things?" (Rom. 8:32).

It is the very nature of God to give. All good things come from above, from his open hand and benevolent heart. Made in his image, we, too, are called to be generous people, extending the goodness of God to others.

We can adopt a lifestyle of giving because God has first given to us. His divine resources are available to us through our relationship with Christ and the presence of the Holy Spirit.

Our first step toward becoming generous people is giving to God. It is our means of acknowledging his lordship and demonstrating our dependence on him. A good beginning is to give a tithe, a tenth of what we earn. This becomes easier when we understand that everything rightfully belongs to God. Returning a fraction of his liberality should delight us. We are to give gleefully, gratefully, humbly.

Obedience in this area enables us to bless others as God honors our commitment. Giving ignites an explosion of divine grace and abundance: "And God is able to make all grace abound to you, so that in all things at all times, having all that you need, you will abound in every good work" (2 Cor. 9:8).

The pump primed by honoring God, pouring forth a torrent of God's spiritual riches, is at our disposal to help others. We can share encouraging words to the discouraged, for we are encouraged by him. We can serve the needs of the emotionally and spiritually impoverished, for he also took on the form of a servant. We can give our friendship to the lonely, for he is our unfailing Friend.

Each act of giving, whatever form it may take, is a divine seed that multiplies our joy and peace. There has never been a time when God did not honor a giving heart. It is a spiritual law for contented, fruitful living in the kingdom of God.

All that we have—salvation, eternal and physical life, and daily sustenance—comes from the Father above. He made you and me so that we could receive his choicest treasure, our relationship with him for eternity.

Our cheerful response should be to imitate him. Give of yourself and your possessions to him and others. Your spirit of generosity will be a fountain of supernatural refreshment to thirsty and needy men and women.

"Give, and it will be given to you" (Luke 6:38).

I can hardly understand your love, heavenly Father. You gave your only Son for my sins, and you continue to give me all that I need each day. Teach me to give of myself to others so that your storehouse of spiritual riches may overflow through me. Do not let me be selfish. Free me from greed so that I may participate in your grand scheme of grace and giving.

TOUCHSTONE

You can never outgive God.

Whoever loves discipline loves knowledge,
but he who hates correction is stupid.

Proverbs 12:1

Don't Be Stupid

*T*he Bible uses the word *stupid* on rare occasions. When it does, we should take heed.

The foolish man in the Scriptures is the one who fails to receive correction. He spurns and ignores it, refusing its counsel. Pride, ego, and plain stubbornness are often the limp excuses for rejecting the reproofs of wisdom.

However, the correction that God gives is actually a remarkable sign of his great love for us. Jesus said, "Those whom I love I rebuke and discipline" (Rev. 3:19).

Like a concerned parent, God corrects his children who are on a wayward path: "The Lord disciplines those he loves, and he punishes everyone he accepts as a son" (Heb. 12:6).

Does that change your view of admonition? Do you see that God's sometimes painful dealings with you are but an extension of his fatherhood? Do you understand that his rebuke only affirms your glorious position as a child of God, who loves you enough to place his disciplining hand on your life?

When you were a child, your mother or father corrected you frequently. Unfortunately, not all of their reprimands were from pure motivations. They probably were angry, upset, or even unjust at times.

This is not the case with the discipline of our heavenly Father. His reproofs are always loving, just, and perfect. He never rebukes us in anger, never seeks to harm us or belittle us. His correction is for our welfare, for our success, for our enlightenment. Because he knows all things, he knows that our unwise actions or thoughts will lead to our eventual destruction; and in his mercy and grace, he intervenes with his kind but firm reproof.

His usual agent of correction is his living Word: "All Scripture is God-breathed and is useful for teaching, rebuking, correcting and training in righteousness" (2 Tim. 3:16). The

Scriptures encourage and guide us, but they frequently do so by pointing out our misconceptions, blunders, and deficiencies.

Our response should be one of immense thanksgiving that through the ministry of his Word God is able to correct our erroneous course. Rather than becoming discouraged, hurt, or combative when God examines us, we should be quick to examine ourselves, repent, and allow the Holy Spirit to direct our steps in his straight path.

God loves you dearly. He is willing to discipline you in order that you may share in his holiness and enjoy the blessings he has in store for the obedient Christian. Don't be "stupid." The rod of God keeps you in his safe pasture and protects you from the consequences of foolish decisions.

I have to confess, Father, that I don't like discipline. Give me discernment to know when you are correcting me. Help me not to pout or become angry, but accept your correction as a demonstration of your love for me.

TOUCHSTONE

*God's correction always steers
us into his love.*

He who walks with the wise grows wise,
but a companion of fools suffers harm.

Proverbs 13:20

The Friendship Factor

My grandfather had a profound influence on my life and ministry. The occasion I had to sit and talk with him about his walk with God not only became a cornerstone in my understanding and relationship with Christ; it also set the direction for my ministry, and I have never wavered from it. It was not what he told me about God that made such an inescapable impression, but what he experienced with God.

Getting to know godly men and women is a choice tool for cultivating the wisdom of God. People who hunger and thirst for God and whose lives exemplify the fruit of the Holy Spirit have much to teach us about the principles of the Scriptures and the character of God. They do not merely possess information about God; they have tested and proved his faithfulness through the years.

If you would like to grow in wisdom, first pray for God to lead you to the persons of his choice to become your close friends. We sometimes think we know best when it comes to establishing Christian friendships. But only God knows the heart, and only God knows who is best equipped to minister to our specific needs and hurts. He knows who can bring God's comfort to us, who can deepen our perspective about his ways, and whose personal experiences can bring his helpful instruction and guidance to our circumstances.

Spiritual maturity is a key. Wisdom is not learned in the course of months or even years. It resides in the one who has endured, who has suffered, who has been sustained by God in times of doubt, adversity, and opposition. This does not mean that spiritual maturity and age always go hand in hand, but it does mean that the individuals you befriend should have some spiritual mileage under their belts.

Look for an encourager. God wants to bless you, to edify you. That may involve correction; but his correction is always given in love and truth, not condemnation. We need to be built up and strengthened in Christ. An encouraging friend seeks our welfare, our good, just as Christ does. He does not overlook our hang-ups, but he motivates us with the good news of God's grace.

The friend who helps us grow in wisdom is also one who hungers and thirsts for God. He is a learner. He is not conceited or prideful and is not afraid to admit his own failures, for we learn from mistakes as well as successes.

Once God directs us to those individuals he has chosen, we need to persevere in our relationships with them. Seek opportunities to spend time with them. There will be all kinds of distractions, but we must "walk with the wise" if we are to become wise.

God-ordained friendships are sharp tools for producing Christlikeness in our lives. You cannot think of David apart from Jonathan; Elisha without Elijah; or Paul without Timothy, Barnabas, or Silas.

Are you learning about God from a wise Christian? It is an adventure that will transform you and prepare you to bring God's truth to others who also need to trust and know him.

Lord, direct me to a friend who will enable me to know you better, one whose walk will inspire me, reprove me, and build me into Christlikeness. Thank you for the people you have already placed in my life and the ones you will direct me to in the future.

TOUCHSTONE

*Godly friends help you draw
near to God.*

A simple man believes anything,
but a prudent man gives thought to his steps.

Proverbs 14:15

Think About It

*O*n many occasions before making important decisions, I ask the Lord this question: "What is the wise thing to do?" While God is ultimately in charge of providing the answer, every believer is responsible for exercising what the Scriptures call "prudence."

Prudence is often used as a synonym for *wisdom*. The prudent man or woman is responsible for using spiritual discernment in practical affairs. The prudent person can avoid unnecessary frustration, failure, and disappointment and can reap the blessings of godly wisdom.

Prudence begins with the gathering of pertinent information. When Moses sent twelve spies into Canaan, he wanted some facts. "What kind of land do they live in? Is it good or bad? What kind of towns do they live in? Are they unwalled or fortified? How is the soil? Is it fertile or poor? Are there trees on it or not?" (Num. 13:19–20). Although God had promised Moses that he would bring the people of Israel into Canaan, Moses was still responsible for appraising the situation wisely.

The purpose for collecting facts is to examine them thoroughly and investigate the information from a godly perspective. We are to sift the facts through the supernatural grid of prayer and God's Word. As we pray about the matter, using the Scriptures as our guide, God works to show us his will and direction. The twelve men brought back an accurate report of the condition of the land and people of Canaan, but ten of them failed to align the facts with God's promise of deliverance.

Like Joshua and Caleb, we must bring the facts before the revealed truth of God's Word. The Word of God sheds supernatural light on our decision-making process. Joshua and Caleb were prudent because they faithfully exercised their task of gathering and analyzing information *and* trusted God for the results.

The prudent person understands that only God knows the

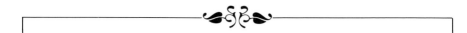

future. We cannot always know all the facts. We cannot forecast the future. However, we can entrust each decision into the sovereign hand of God. Joshua and Caleb knew the promise of God to deliver them from the giant residents of Canaan, but they had to trust him to fulfill his pledge.

Prudence is doing all we can to make responsible, wise decisions while placing our complete faith in God's providence and faithfulness. When we do so, we can count on God's encouraging and faith-building direction.

Father, I don't often look before I leap. My landings are not pretty. Help me to take the time to look things over thoroughly when making important decisions. Let me know what you want, and I will trust you for the outcome.

TOUCHSTONE

Always ask, "What is the wise thing to do?"

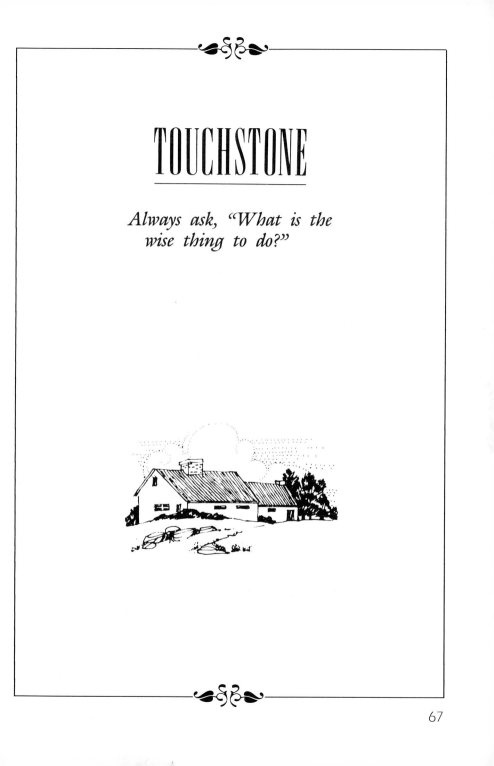

The Lord is far from the wicked
but he hears the prayer of the righteous.

Proverbs 15:29

Is Anybody Listening?

*D*oes God hear your prayers?

David wrote that if he "had cherished sin in [his] heart, the Lord would not have listened" (Ps. 66:18). James said that our prayers can be powerful and effective, but they must come from a "righteous" person (James 5:16).

Doesn't that count us out? Don't we all secretly harbor sin of one sort or another in our souls? And if the competence of our prayer life is based on the degree of our righteousness, do we not all fall short?

If our response to these questions is based on our own feelings or spiritual effort, we would have to conclude that God seldom hears our prayers and that the prayers that do reach the Father are weak. However, when we understand the radical good news of the Gospel, we can joyfully declare that God hears our every word, is intimately acquainted with every thought, and is eager to respond to the slightest utterance of our heart or lips.

Here's why. The cross of Christ, the pivotal point and cornerstone of eternity, provided the divine answer to both of these dilemmas. At Calvary, our sin was forgiven, not just our past sins before we were saved but all of our sins—past, present, and future. We are a forgiven people. There is no need for false guilt or condemnation. Confession is still essential to keeping your relationship with Christ intimate, but your sins can never keep you from enjoying your eternal position as a forgiven child of God. Your sin account with God is cleared, settled by the death of Christ. Your sins, all of them, have been carried away by Christ. If the Holy Spirit convicts you of a specific sin, agree that it is an offense to God, repent, and move on.

Better yet, in the cross of Christ God not only forgave you all your sins, but he also attributed the righteousness of Christ to you. Sin was taken away, and the righteousness of God was credited to you. You do not work to attain that righteousness,

you simply received it by faith when you accepted Jesus as your Savior.

Righteousness is a condition of unending acceptability by God. You will never be more righteous than you are right now. At the core of your identity in Christ you are completely righteous, holy, and blameless. You can never become unrighteous or rejected because of your behavior. You may be disciplined or chastened by God if you sin, but God will never change your status as his righteous child.

The prayers of a righteous person are heard; and that is what you are, the righteousness of God in Christ Jesus (2 Cor. 5:21). Pray fervently. Pray always. God's ear is continually open to the cry of the righteous, and your sins are cast into the depths of the sea.

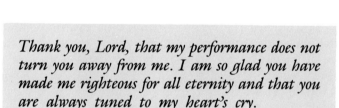

Thank you, Lord, that my performance does not turn you away from me. I am so glad you have made me righteous for all eternity and that you are always tuned to my heart's cry.

TOUCHSTONE

You are as righteous in Christ today as you ever will be.

Whoever gives heed to instruction prospers,
and blessed is he who trusts in the Lord.

Proverbs 16:20

Leaning on Jesus

I observed a man repairing lines on a telephone pole outside my home one day. Despite the height, he worked with apparent ease and dispatch, securely leaning his entire weight on a thick leather safety belt.

That is what trusting the Lord is like. We go about our appointed rounds at work and at home, tackling an assortment of tasks. On the surface, it may appear that we work in our own sufficiency; but we realize that our spiritual success depends on leaning our emotional, spiritual, and volitional weight on the Lord Jesus Christ. He is the source of our strength and security. We are dependent on him. Our times are in his hands.

Trusting in the Lord, leaning on his adequacy, is possible as we anchor our confidence in the promises of God. There are some fearful moments in life, times when we doubt, times of confusion and anxiety. Then, when circumstances are less than favorable, nothing is more comforting or stabilizing than looking to the Scriptures for support and direction. God's Word is sure. It never fails—not one word. It ministers to our deepest needs and speaks to our innermost being. When we place our faith in God's Word, we accept it as his truth, despite our wavering feelings. We simply believe that God means what he says and that he will fulfill all his promises.

We also lean our weight on Christ by affirming the character of God. We can trust in his Word because he is trustworthy. We can count on his help because he is faithful. The attributes of God—such as his holiness, goodness, mercy, justice, and grace—anchor our faith in him. The better we know him, the more we trust him. The more we trust him, the more we see his hand at work in our midst.

Perhaps one of the most significant ways that we place our full trust in Christ is by praising him regardless of the circumstances. Praise shouts our faith in God. It exalts him and declares that we will follow him and look to him even when the

odds appear against us. As we praise God, we magnify the majesty and greatness of our Father. We focus on who God is, and that is a divinely given catalyst for trusting him still more. Praise drives away fear and builds faith.

The person who trusts in the Lord is blessed. He clings to the promises of God, delights in the character of God, and worships God in darkness or in light. He leans on the everlasting arms that never fail or forsake him.

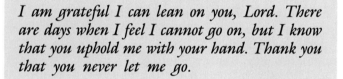

I am grateful I can lean on you, Lord. There are days when I feel I cannot go on, but I know that you uphold me with your hand. Thank you that you never let me go.

TOUCHSTONE

When you lean on Jesus, your footing is always firm.

He who covers over an offense promotes love.

Proverbs 17:9

An Upward Promotion

*M*any believers are good record-keepers. They tend to tally the offenses of others against them, keeping an up-to-date emotional track record of their hurts. The unfortunate sum of such tabulations is strife, anger, bitterness, and resentment.

The way of wisdom in dealing with those who wrong us is the way of love. Jesus' work of reconciliation on the cross destroyed any record of our sins against God. "God was reconciling the world to himself in Christ, not counting men's sins against them" (2 Cor. 5:19). God no longer keeps any summary sheet of our wrongs. He has chosen instead to forgive us when we, by faith, receive the gift of his Son, Jesus Christ.

Who are we, then, to harbor grudges against those who wound us? If Jesus, whom all sin is ultimately against, has covered our sins with his cleansing love, how can we fail to extend his love to others?

How does God love us? Unconditionally. Without strings. Without limit. How are we to love others? The same way, according to the apostle Paul. Christian love "keeps no record of wrongs" (1 Cor. 13:5). When you choose to forgive another his offense against you, you erase the mental tally sheet of his trespass. It is possible that you may not forget—but, like God, you choose not to hold the offender in emotional debt to you.

How do you extend such love? When we experience the extraordinary, forgiving love of God because Christ died for us, we express the healing power of that love by dying to self. We choose to die to our rights. We deliberately decide in obedience to Christ and his Word to forfeit any right of retaliation or revenge. Only then is the love of God able to be released by the power of the Holy Spirit. Is it difficult? It certainly is. Does it happen without a struggle? Almost never. But it does enable us to forgive others as Christ has forgiven us.

Promoting love does not come naturally to us, but it is the very nature of our God, who is Love and who is our Life. Each time we release his love through an act of forgiveness, we extend the same grace he has given to us and continues to give. "Do not repay evil with evil or insult with insult, but with blessing, because to this you were called so you may inherit a blessing" (1 Peter 3:9). Be a blessing and inherit the peace, joy, and righteousness of the kingdom of God by promoting his love to those who hurt you.

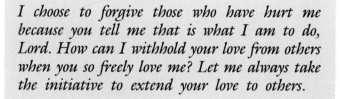

I choose to forgive those who have hurt me because you tell me that is what I am to do, Lord. How can I withhold your love from others when you so freely love me? Let me always take the initiative to extend your love to others.

TOUCHSTONE

Each time you forgive, you
choose freedom in Christ.

He who answers before listening—
that is his folly and his shame.

Proverbs 18:13

God Is Still Speaking

*F*or forty-seven years I have been a follower of Christ. One of the most practical, exciting, and rewarding lessons has been learning to listen to God. It is the key to knowing him and walking in his will. It is absolutely essential to an intimate relationship with Christ, which should be the goal of every believer.

Cultivating the essential art of listening is a vital discipline for developing godly wisdom. Practical James wrote that "everyone should be quick to listen, slow to speak and slow to become angry" (James 1:19). His admonition obviously cuts across our natural grain of freely expressing our own opinions, whether we are asked for them or not, and underscores God's desire to heighten our receptivity to himself and others.

Listening to God is crucial for a mature Christian walk. God is still speaking today because he wants to communicate his will and love to us just as much as he did to the people of Bible times. We hear his voice primarily through his Word. The Holy Spirit impresses a verse or providentially arranges circumstances so that we may hear, see, and experience the wonder of his guidance and provision.

God also speaks to us through the wisdom of other people. He is at work in all of his obedient children who bring God's Word of encouragement or enlightenment at just the right moment. How important, then, that we learn to let others share with us, to adopt the position of a hearer. The Scriptures tell us we are to consider others better than ourselves (Phil. 2:3). That doesn't mean only those Christians who are impressive, but all believers. God can use the most lowly of his children, even a child, to communicate his will.

However, hearing God speak is difficult to the one intent on merely making his own petitions known. We must be quiet in our spirit, at rest in our souls, asking God to speak clearly to us through his Word. Nothing compares to the thrill of knowing

that God has spoken directly to our particular circumstances. His speaking through his Word in this way is an expression of his love and care in every detail of our lives.

Listening carefully to God and other Christians allows us to have the full input of supernatural revelation before making decisions. It places us in the humble posture of a learner who desires above all to hear the voice of God. God is still speaking. Are you listening?

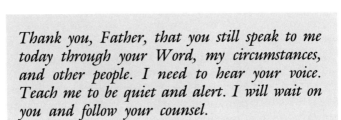

Thank you, Father, that you still speak to me today through your Word, my circumstances, and other people. I need to hear your voice. Teach me to be quiet and alert. I will wait on you and follow your counsel.

TOUCHSTONE

Listening to God is the way of wisdom.

A man's wisdom gives him patience.

Proverbs 19:11

Perfect Timing

R ight timing is critical. It is crucial for success in warfare, in science, in sports, in business deals, in relationships, and in just about any other endeavor of everyday living. But did you know that right timing is equally significant in your spiritual walk? And did you know that God requires your timely cooperation with him to fulfill his plan for you?

Almost invariably, discovering and cooperating with God's perfect timing requires waiting on him. We are impatient creatures. We become easily frustrated, irritated, and often discouraged when we encounter obstacles that delay or hinder us. But God is always on time, never late. He is never thwarted by any circumstance; and when we choose to wait for his timing, we position ourselves for God's maximum blessing.

Waiting on God is not an irksome, boring task. It is one of the most exciting activities a believer can participate in because the rewards are so incredible. It is not a passive attitude but a dynamic expectation, as we focus our attention through persistent prayer and meditation on God's Word. It is a deliberate setting of the mind, heart, and will to know and do the will of the Father at all costs. It is a matter of rejecting our fear of failure, refusing to yield to the unwise opinions of others, and steadfastly resisting the urge to move recklessly ahead when we are unsure of God's plan.

When we foolishly launch out on our timetable instead of God's, we miss God's best for our lives. The prophet Samuel told King Saul to wait for him at Gilgal for seven days. When Samuel did not show, Saul felt compelled to offer the burnt offering himself and thus forfeited his kingship over Israel. Consequently, God decided to find a man after his own heart (1 Sam. 13:12–14). That man was David, who, more than any other author of Scripture, wrote about waiting on God. David acknowledged God's plan and timing for his life by refusing to take advantage of two opportunities to slay Saul. After Saul was killed by his own

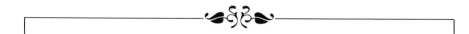

sword, David became the king of Judah. However, he waited on God for seven more years before the men of Israel asked him to reign over them as well. When he became their king, David could confidently say that he "knew that the LORD had established him as king over Israel" (2 Sam. 5:12).

When we wait for God's perfect timing, we *know* that God has directed us and blessed us. We taste of his goodness and grace. We have the sheer joy of experiencing God's magnificent care and provision. We see his answer to prayer. We discover his good and perfect will. We know God is working on our behalf. We win the battles of life by waiting steadfastly on God, who accomplishes all things on our behalf. Wait patiently on him in every circumstance, and you will be a person after God's own heart. There is no higher blessing.

I am quick to get ahead of you, Father. I am so impatient. Teach me to wait on you without being passive. I have many things to do, but nothing is more important than waiting for your timing.

TOUCHSTONE

God is never late.

A man's steps are directed by the Lord.
How then can anyone understand his own way?

Proverbs 20:24

Under Construction

I watched some interstate road construction with great interest recently. A small overpass that had been built in the beginning phases of construction appeared hopelessly disconnected to the entire project. There were no roads leading to or from the overpass; it was just a span of concrete that seemed to lead nowhere. However, when the project was completed, the seemingly misplaced overpass proved to be a vital link at a heavily traveled interstate junction.

Sometimes our lives can seem a bit like that. We are not sure why we are working at that particular job, living in this particular city, or attending this particular school. We simply do not see how it fits into God's scheme of things.

It is exactly at this juncture that we must rely on the sovereignty of God. God knows what he desires to accomplish in our lives. He is aware of how this day, this job, this relationship is pieced together in his good and acceptable plan. You see, our wisdom has limits. We do not know what a day will bring forth. However, God's wisdom is infinite and transcendent. He weaves every thread of our existence into a purposeful, productive, profitable plan.

When I decided many years ago to come to First Baptist Church of Atlanta, I was pastoring a growing, thriving church, and I was perfectly content there. I was not sure why I should move, but I knew God was directing me to do so.

The first few years in Atlanta were intensely stressful. However, we steadily grew, and God opened a small door for the *In Touch* broadcast. Today these broadcasts can be heard worldwide.

More than twenty years ago, I could never have foreseen either the struggles or the successes of this ministry. I simply obeyed God and trusted him. And that is the key to bringing order and meaning to what seems like chaotic, meaningless seasons in our lives. Somehow Joseph understood that principle

several thousand years ago. At age seventeen he enjoyed the prosperity of a prominent Hebrew family. For the next thirteen years, he worked as a servant in a foreign land and spent time in an Egyptian jail. In each experience, though, Joseph's steady hand and diligence caused him to find favor with God. He did the best with what he had, did what he knew to be right, and trusted God. He did not know at seventeen years of age that he would administer the Egyptian kingdom at thirty.

God uses *everything* for good in your life when you entrust yourself and your circumstances to his providential control. No situation is hopeless. No problem is outside his love, wisdom, or sovereignty. You may not understand the present state of your life, but God does. Rest in his sufficiency and sovereignty.

I must confess, Lord, that there are seasons in my life that seem futile. When I don't understand, it is comforting and reassuring to know that you have a purpose for everything in my life. Thank you for your sovereignty.

TOUCHSTONE

God is in control.

The king's heart is in the hand of the Lord;
he directs it like a watercourse wherever he pleases.

Proverbs 21:1

Major and Minor Decisions

When facing major or minor decisions in life, I always ask, "What would obedience to God require of me?" My choice must never be based on the possible outcome of my decision, but rather on what God would have me do. That requires me to place my own will in neutral so that God can move me in his direction. It also requires me to be cautious in listening to the many voices of counsel that may be contrary to his guidance. Like everyone else, I am prone to give undue emphasis to particular pieces of information or words of counsel.

Our "heart is in the hand of the Lord" when we are fully surrendered to Jesus Christ as Lord. Jesus is our Savior, Lord, and Life. He asks for total submission of our total being to him. Surrender has negative connotations in our society. It is usually coupled with defeat and weakness. However, in the spiritual realm, surrender is always linked to victory and success. It is the means by which we confess that God knows what is best for us as we yield our rights to him. It is the acceptance of his lordship. When I tell Jesus that I truly want his wisdom and his will, I become clay in the Potter's hand, a sheep of his pasture, dependent on him for guidance and protection.

The surrendered heart is also a sifted heart. I allow God to sift my motivations. Do I really want to honor and glorify Christ in this matter, or am I seeking to exalt myself? "All a man's ways seem right to him, but the LORD weighs the heart" (Prov. 21:2). This process of sifting strains out selfish or impure motives. I begin to delight myself in the Lord. The desires of my heart become conformed with his plans.

At this point, I am conscious of my need for the Holy Spirit's help. Just as the Holy Spirit led Paul on his missionary journeys, sending him to specific towns and people, he leads and

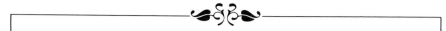

teaches us today. He is our sure and divine Guide who will steer us into God's truth. We can count on his enlightenment.

Once convinced that I am surrendered to God, that my motives are right, and that I have sought the Holy Spirit's help, I step out in obedience to the will of God as I perceive it. He can correct me or redirect me at any point—"wherever he pleases." I am trusting in him with all my heart and not leaning on my own understanding. I am his obedient child. God is fully responsible for those who fully commit themselves to him, and I know that he has taken me under his care and will not fail or forsake me.

Jesus, thank you that you desire that I know your will even more than I desire it. You are the Good Shepherd who guides his flock. I look to you as my Guide. Teach me the way in which I should go.

TOUCHSTONE

We need guidance, and we have the right Guide.

The sluggard says, "There is a lion outside!"
or, "I will be murdered in the streets!"

Proverbs 22:13

Excuses, Excuses

*W*hen we delay that important phone call, put off necessary chores around the house, postpone our medical examination, delay making things right with an offended friend, fail to spend time in the Word with the Lord, whatever our excuse, the truth is we are practicing the subtle art of procrastination.

Like the sluggard in Proverbs, we invent any number of excuses to delay crucial decisions or put off simple tasks. Nevertheless, procrastination is a form of bondage that is more costly than any of us would like to admit.

Some of us practice procrastination as a means of what I term "discomfort dodging." Our goal is not to feel bad, and we steadfastly avoid anything that has the potential of generating anxiety. We do not want to leave our comfort zone. When the apostle Paul presented the Gospel to Felix, a Roman governor, Felix "was afraid and said, 'That's enough for now! You may leave. When I find it convenient, I will send for you'" (Acts 24:25). Like Felix, we tend to postpone those circumstances that make us uneasy.

We also procrastinate because of a sense of inadequacy or a fear of failure. We might not succeed. We may very well blunder and embarrass ourselves; so why try in the first place? It is far easier to remain stationary and stay within our perceived capabilities than venture into risky endeavors. We doubt ourselves. As a result, important tasks are left undone; we deprive God of a vessel through which he desires to work. We experience nagging feelings of guilt, and our spiritual growth is stunted.

The first step for you to take if God is to deliver you from the bondage of procrastination is to admit your problem. Confess that you do make unnecessary excuses to avoid certain people or tasks. Once you admit you have the problem, ask God's forgiveness. He wants you to enjoy an abundant life and is willing to help you with any problem that hinders you from experiencing his fullness.

Then, by an act of faith, choose to live your life based on who you are in Christ Jesus rather than on your feelings of inadequacy or self-doubt. Believe that you *can* do all things through Christ who strengthens you for every task and makes you equal to every challenge (Phil. 4:13). Trust in the Lord with *all* your heart. He is your sufficiency. If you fail, move on and try and again. The truth is, you will find yourself succeeding far more than you imagined and discovering the reality of God's equipping power. The captivity of procrastination will be broken; and you will be able to face any situation with the sure knowledge that God is with you, for you, and in you. You are not on your own, and he will not fail you. Make this your motto: "Do it now."

Show me any areas of my life where I may be procrastinating and making excuses. Teach me to trust you and not look to my inadequate resources but to your abundant provision. Thank you for equipping me for every challenge.

TOUCHSTONE

Do it now!

Do not wear yourself out to get rich;
have the wisdom to show restraint.

Proverbs 23:4

Money Management

*M*oney is not primarily a financial issue for the Christian. Certainly, we are to live under budgetary constraints and use money wisely; but for the believer, money is fundamentally a spiritual issue. What matters is not how we view money but how God views it. When we approach it from his perspective, then the management of our finances is governed by spiritual principles, not cultural trends.

The bottom line for understanding money from a spiritual vantage point is this: God owns it all. It is God who created the heavens and the earth. It is God who created humankind. By right of creation, God is the sole owner of the universe and its enormous wealth. "'The silver is mine and the gold is mine,' declares the LORD Almighty" (Hag. 2:8). God gives us the health, wisdom, life, and strength to make money. While we may sharpen our skills through education, God provides us with all the raw material for accumulating income. Money is not evil. Wealth is not sinful. But whether we work for it, invest it, save it, or give it away, all our wealth belongs to the Lord Jesus Christ.

That puts the matter of our finances into an entirely new perspective. Since God is the sole owner of our resources, our responsibility is simply to manage what he entrusts to us. We are stewards of his riches. Our paycheck, our investments, our bank account—little or big—are to be administered under the guidance of practical scriptural principles.

God's Word tells us that poor managers of a little money will be poor managers of much money. If we are faithful in using our present treasures responsibly and obediently, God will entrust additional finances into our care. Faithfully handling your finances means you avoid the worldly snare of competing with others. It means that you are to be content with what God provides, concentrating on the very real rewards that come from being rich in good works. It means that giving God at least a tenth of your income will be a priority, not an option. It means

that you will do everything possible to avoid the debt trap and its bondage. There are hundreds of Scriptures that give God's viewpoint on money, and they will revolutionize the way you handle your finances.

Money will never satisfy completely. It was not meant to be an idol but merely a medium of exchange. It is not something we place our confidence in. Rather, our trust is wholly in God, who supplies all our needs according to his riches in glory.

Evaluating money from God's viewpoint will prevent us from squandering our time and talents on the relentless pursuit of wealth. It will liberate us instead to seek God's mind and wisdom and enjoy the superabundance of living by his unchanging, profitable principles.

I choose to pursue you, Lord, not wealth. Since you own it all, you will give me what I need as I depend on you. Let my finances be ordered by you and not by my impulses. I look forward to the freedom you will bring in this area as I obey you.

TOUCHSTONE

God owns it all.

By wisdom a house is built,
and through understanding it is established;
through knowledge its rooms are filled
with rare and beautiful treasures.

Proverbs 24:3–4

The House Built on the Rock

*T*he home is the greenhouse where godly wisdom is cultivated. The power of consistent Christian living in the context of family relationships is the primary spiritual classroom for authentic Christianity. The home is where the majority of behavioral traits—good and bad—are learned, reinforced, and passed along to future generations.

God's wisdom fills the home when acceptance of each member is faithfully practiced. Did you know that each member of your family, whether saved or not, is of great worth to God? All your family members have been created by him and are greatly loved by him. Their value is inestimable in his eyes, and he desires that everyone know him. Do you accept your mate, your children, your in-laws, your grandchildren just as they are, or do you love them only when they meet your performance standards? Paul wrote, "Accept one another, then, just as Christ accepted you" (Rom. 15:7). How does Christ accept you? Unconditionally. How should you accept the members of your family? In the same way.

A companion of acceptance is accountability to God. Parents must provide loving limits for their children, but every family member is ultimately accountable to God for his or her actions. Understanding and applying this truth teaches the children to seek to know God's mind and learn that their primary task is to obey him. Obeying mom and dad then becomes simply an expression of their desire to please and follow God. Husband and wife are freed from the bondage of selfish desires in order to rightly esteem one another.

A home is also filled with fragrant and appealing spiritual riches when each family member adopts a servant's spirit. Most family arguments and dissension stem from a failure to yield

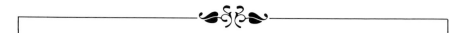

personal rights. A person filled with the Spirit of Christ strongly desires to serve. He does not seek to establish his own emotional turf but freely edifies and encourages other family members through his servant spirit.

Practice these spiritual disciplines in your home. Accept other family members as they are and let God change them according to his plan for their lives. Be accountable to God and obey him. Serve one another gladly. As you do, your home will be a divine display of God's gentle and enduring wisdom.

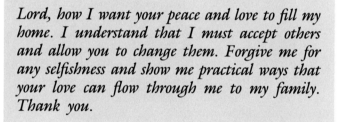

Lord, how I want your peace and love to fill my home. I understand that I must accept others and allow you to change them. Forgive me for any selfishness and show me practical ways that your love can flow through me to my family. Thank you.

TOUCHSTONE

Fill your house with the treasure of wisdom.

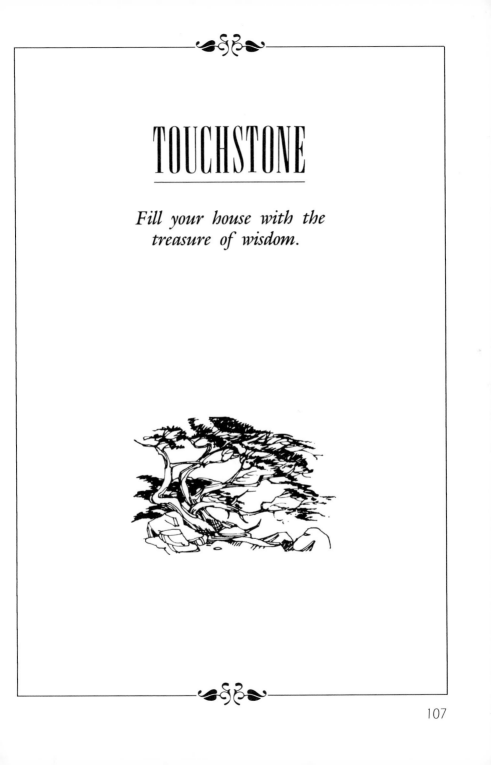

*Like a city whose walls are broken down
is a man who lacks self-control.*

Proverbs 25:28

Controlling Your Thoughts

*I*n ancient civilizations, the primary defense for cities was huge, imposing walls. Once the walls were surmounted, victory for the aggressor was virtually ensured.

The Scriptures compare a person without self-control to such a ravaged city. He is at the mercy of external forces, subject to double-mindedness. He is tossed to and fro by turbulent emotions and passions. His life is unstable and only occasionally fruitful.

The key to developing self-control with a spiritual emphasis is not more self-determination. It is not a doubling of efforts or better time management. The pivotal discipline for gaining godly self-control is the renewing of the mind. Like the ancient walls, the mind is the crucial defense mechanism. If it is broached by negative, critical, undisciplined thoughts, our behavior and our entire personality are adversely affected. We act out the way we perceive ourselves, the way we think. Our actions conform with our thinking. Right thinking is the first step toward right living.

We renew our minds and exhibit the godly fruit of self-control and other biblical traits by first understanding our position in Christ. Our position in Christ is our relationship with him. We have been crucified with him. We were buried with him and raised with him. We are now seated with him in the heavenly places. He is living on the inside of us through the Holy Spirit.

We can control our thinking, and thus our behavior, through the knowledge of our identity in Christ. We are new creatures, saints, holy and blameless in him. When Satan assaults the walls of our minds with alluring enticements, we do not have to yield, because of who we are in Christ. He is the source of our strength. He is our life.

Since Christ is now your life and you are in him, it makes

good sense to "set your [mind] on things above, not on earthly things" (Col. 3:2). Our thinking is in keeping with our position in Christ. We concentrate on the things that are true, right, pure, noble, lovely, admirable, praiseworthy, and excellent (Phil. 4:8). We view things from God's perspective.

"How can I do that?" you ask. Well, when I was young, people ordered many items from a catalog. They had never seen the items except as they were pictured in the catalog. The Scriptures are our catalog. We know what setting our minds on heavenly things is like because God's Word reveals his mind to us.

Does that mean we ignore our earthly responsibilities? Of course not. However, we seek God's kingdom first, allowing his priorities and his ways to saturate our thinking. We realize that we are here primarily to glorify him; and as we do, he promises to take care of our daily necessities, leading us into a more intimate walk with him as we go about our tasks.

The godly fruit of self-control comes as the Holy Spirit works by his power to renew our minds. It is then that our behavior is transformed.

I understand that my mind is a battleground, Lord. Only as you renew my mind can I win the war. Don't let me be led astray by feeling, but continually remind me of who I am in you.

TOUCHSTONE

The way you perceive yourself determines your actions.

As charcoal to embers and as wood to fire,
so is a quarrelsome man for kindling strife.

Proverbs 26:21

A Gentle Spirit

A man loves what God loves and hates what God hates. Although God hates all sin, he greatly detests the evil of spreading "dissension among brothers" (Prov. 6:19). God is opposed to all forms of quarreling and bickering—evils that spread hostility and anger.

The cure for strife is a gentle spirit. A gentle spirit is not feminine or masculine. It is a divinely given spirit, which pervades our hearts through the supernatural activity of the Holy Spirit. It is an inner adornment that should characterize every follower of Jesus Christ, the One who described himself as "gentle and humble in heart" (Matt. 11:29).

A gentle person is a peacemaker. He does not want peace at any cost, but he does nothing to unduly offend or disturb another. He speaks firmly and confidently but not arrogantly. He appreciates the worth of others as God's handiwork. His gentleness is revealed in his actions and his words. "A gentle answer turns away wrath, but a harsh word stirs up anger" (Prov. 15:1).

A gentle person is an effective tool in Christ's hand in almost every relationship. The gentle spouse shows the love of God to his or her mate. The gentle worker demonstrates the reality of Christ's compassion in a cold and harsh workplace. Even when others belligerently attack our faith in God, we are to respond clearly but with "gentleness and respect" (1 Peter 3:15). A godly, gentle spirit is a visible testimony of the character of God to believer and unbeliever alike.

Isn't it interesting that when God spoke to the prophet Elijah in the Old Testament, his voice was not dramatically loud. It was not in the mighty wind or the forceful earthquake that he revealed himself, but in the "gentle whisper" (1 Kings 19:12). God desires that we too speak in a gentle voice.

Ask Christ to fill you daily with the Holy Spirit. Rest in him. Abide in him. The divine sap of God's gentle Spirit will flow

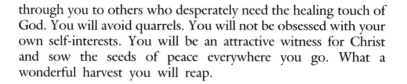

through you to others who desperately need the healing touch of God. You will avoid quarrels. You will not be obsessed with your own self-interests. You will be an attractive witness for Christ and sow the seeds of peace everywhere you go. What a wonderful harvest you will reap.

Lord, your gentleness was so evident as you ministered on earth. You were kind to all who sought your help. Through your Spirit implant in me your gentleness. Keep me away from strife and make me a peacemaker.

TOUCHSTONE

*Christ in you is the gentle
Lamb of God.*

The crucible for silver and the furnace for gold,
but man is tested by the praise he receives.

Proverbs 27:21

The Test of Success

Success can be just as much of a spiritual proving ground as adversity. In fact, many who endure the darkness of trials fail in the glow of success. God uses our response to the praises of others to reveal and expose the bent of our hearts.

Handling success properly begins with a right estimation of ourselves. God is the source of all our talents and energies. The glory is his. But we are his instruments, his workmanship. When our deeds earn the approval of others, we can be gracious and thankful. There is no need for false humility.

The apostle Paul put it this way: "Do not think of yourself more highly than you ought, but rather think of yourself with sober judgment, in accordance with the measure of faith God has given you" (Rom. 12:3). We are not worms. We are not simpletons. God has given each of us a sound mind and equipped us to honor him in our appointed tasks. We can humbly receive the appreciation of others while still acknowledging God.

Paul understood the tension that personal praise can bring. When God used Paul to heal a lame man, the people began to worship him. However, Paul pointed their attention to the true God. In Corinth, Paul put out another fire of personal adulation when he discovered that some of the Corinthians were following him rather than Christ.

The subtle appeal of success is always to enlarge our self-esteem and magnify our importance. Notice that I said "enlarge" and "magnify." A person with proper self-esteem rightly values his own worth as God's handiwork but realizes the awesome power and majesty of his Maker. Any praise that is accorded him only serves to stimulate his worship of such a magnificent Father.

When others publicly notice you, receive their appreciation and then take a few moments in private to thank our heavenly Father. That is what Jesus did. After he performed several of his miracles and the crowds gathered, he withdrew for a season of private fellowship with the heavenly Father.

Make sure that you do not praise or exalt yourself. "Let another praise you, and not your own mouth" (Prov. 27:2). Accept the congratulations of others, give glory to God, keep your eyes on your Source—Jesus Christ—and you will pass the test of praise.

Heavenly Father, I enjoy success, but do not let it draw me away from you. Keep my focus right so that when others praise me, I can receive their approval without expanding my ego. Keep me alert to the dangers of success by keeping me close to you.

TOUCHSTONE

Seek to please God, and the praise of others will be kept in proper perspective.

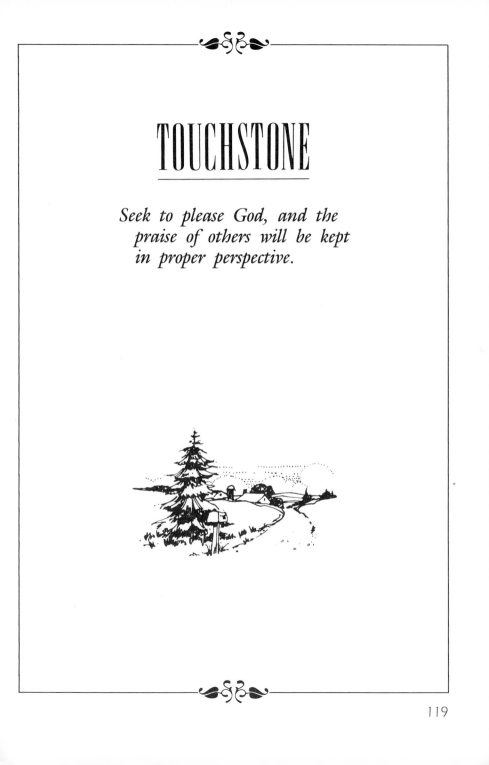

The righteous are as bold as a lion.

Proverbs 28:1

Gaining Confidence

*A*re you a confident Christian? Is your relationship with Jesus Christ characterized by a growing boldness, or are you somewhat tentative and timid? While the believer is to walk humbly before God, he should also express great confidence in his great God.

We can be confident in the purpose of God. His purpose is to conform us to the image of his Son, Jesus Christ; and he *will* finish that objective. We can be "confident of this, that he who began a good work in [us] will carry it on to completion until the day of Christ Jesus" (Phil. 1:6). As we cooperate with the Father on earth, we are transformed into his image. The comforting news is that he accomplishes this by his Spirit and by his grace. We are not left to our own devices or cleverness. In heaven the job will be finished, for God always completes what he begins.

We can be confident in presenting our petitions to the Father. We are to come boldly into God's presence and there present our needs and burdens. He promises that he will hear and answer us according to his love and wisdom. The shed blood of Jesus Christ has paved our way into the throne room of God. We need not be afraid, for he is our Friend. We need not feel guilty, for all our sins are forgiven. We come to a throne of mercy and grace. When we ask according to his will, he assures us that we will receive his gracious and timely reply. "This is the confidence we have in approaching God: that if we ask anything according to his will, he hears us. And if we know that he hears us—whatever we ask—we know that we have what we asked of him" (1 John 5:14–15).

Our confidence is also in the promises of God. God's Word is living and powerful. Peter wrote that God "has given us his very great and precious promises, so that through them you may participate in the divine nature" (2 Peter 1:4). The Scriptures are God's very personal word to you. You can count on a promise from God. He will fulfill his Word in his way, in his timing; he

always keeps his promises. When you place your faith in the truths of the Scriptures, you will never be disappointed. Each time you trust in his Word you experience the reality of his truth.

If you are lacking confidence, ponder these truths. They will encourage you, sustain you, and strengthen your inner self. You will mount up on eagles' wings and face life with great assurance in the incredible goodness of God.

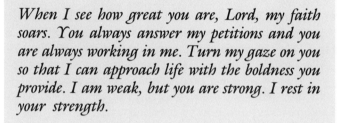

When I see how great you are, Lord, my faith soars. You always answer my petitions and you are always working in me. Turn my gaze on you so that I can approach life with the boldness you provide. I am weak, but you are strong. I rest in your strength.

TOUCHSTONE

*The more we magnify God,
the smaller our problems
appear.*

Fear of man will prove to be a snare,
but whoever trusts in the Lord is kept safe.

Proverbs 29:25

Pulling Down Strongholds

*F*ear is a major stronghold in the hearts of many Christians. I talk with people who are afraid of so many things—afraid of losing control, afraid of the future, afraid of other people. Some live in a constant state of worry.

The antidote for fear is a fixed focus of faith on the Person of Jesus Christ. As long as we dwell on anxious circumstances, turning them constantly over in our minds, we will likely remain in emotional turmoil. However, when we choose—and it is an act of the will—to focus on Jesus Christ, our fearful feelings can and will gradually diminish.

That may sound too easy. I do not want to make light of your fears, for they are very real. Nonetheless, I want to encourage you to place your trust in Jesus Christ. It is really the only means to put your fears in perspective and pull down the strongholds of anxiety.

You can overcome your fears because God *knows* about your circumstances. He is not distant or far off. He is in you, so he is keenly aware of the factors that generate fear. Peace can begin to replace fear when you realize that the God of heaven and earth is intimately aware of your needs and problems.

It is comforting to understand that God knows about our fears, but it is even more encouraging to grasp that he *cares*. Jesus Christ is your personal Shepherd who cares for his flock. Night and day he works to administer his love, grace, mercy, and help to you. He loves you. He delights in you. He wanted to share his life with you so much that he came to earth and died in your place. That is how much he cares. He will spare nothing to aid you. He will withhold no good thing from you.

Not only is God aware of your fears and concerned for your well-being, but he is also *able* to bring about change. God is in

control. There is no situation that he cannot handle. There is no circumstance producing fear that he is not able to work out for your welfare. The power of God is available to help you. There is nothing too difficult for him.

God knows. God cares. God is able. Put all of your trust in Jesus Christ. Tell him about your fears and then choose to place your focus and faith in the loving hands of your loving God.

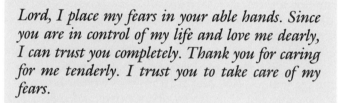

Lord, I place my fears in your able hands. Since you are in control of my life and love me dearly, I can trust you completely. Thank you for caring for me tenderly. I trust you to take care of my fears.

TOUCHSTONE

Remove fear with a fixed focus of faith on Jesus Christ.

Ants are creatures of little strength,
yet they store up their food in the summer.

Proverbs 30:25

What Are You Living For?

I often find that people with limited resources or time can accomplish far more than individuals with far greater talents. The key to their achievements in most cases is diligent planning. Planning is simply making preparations today for tomorrow's opportunities.

When we read the New Testament, it becomes obvious that the apostle Paul had a distinct plan for spreading the Gospel. He visited the leading cities of various provinces, realizing that the Gospel's influence would spread to other communities. It is likewise apparent that God had a plan of salvation, the plan to send his Son to die for our sins. He conceived this plan even before the creation of the universe.

The key to good planning is good goal setting. Goals are written, clearly understood objectives that we arrive at after careful thought and prayer. The only really rewarding goal setting comes after we have asked God to search our hearts for any improper motives and surrendered our wills to his. Once we do these things, we are free to establish goals that are measurable, honest, reasonable, and clear. Ask yourself the following questions: "Can I honestly ask God's help in striving to reach this goal?" "Will it help someone else reach his or her goal?" "Will it violate my conscience?" "Am I willing to pay the price to succeed?"

You will find this process easier if you divide your goals for various sectors of your life—spiritual, family, vocational, and social. Write down as many goals as you feel are necessary. Ask God for discernment as to which goals may not be according to his will. Be flexible and review your goals from time to time, making adjustments as God guides. You may find that you

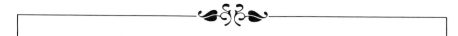

understated your goals in some areas and overstated them in others.

Many years ago my wife and I spent a week setting goals for our personal life, the family, and our ministry. I can honestly say that week was one of the most important of my life. God gave me a tiny glimpse of what our future could hold if we would only trust him and follow the plan he was giving us. I have seen God fulfill many of these goals ahead of my expected schedule and in the most remarkable ways. Most important, my faith in God has grown by leaps and bounds. I now understand more clearly what an awesome God we serve.

As you pray and plan, setting goals under God's leadership, your faith will also grow and you will be used to the maximum of your potential.

Lord, I desire to accomplish your will. I understand that setting goals is a realistic way for me to achieve your purposes. I choose to set aside the time to pray and think about your objectives for my life. I am trusting you to enable me to reach my potential.

TOUCHSTONE

*Set your goals and live
by faith.*

Charm is deceptive, and beauty is fleeting;
but a woman who fears the Lord is to be praised.
                                        Proverbs 31:30

A Virtuous Woman

A godly woman is a great treasure. She is a gift from the Lord and is to be received and treated with great dignity. The description of the virtuous woman in Proverbs 31 is one of the most beautiful descriptions of womankind in all of literature.

The most important aspect of the godly woman is her character: "A wife of noble character who can find?" (Prov. 31:10). Our culture concentrates on physical appearance. We are more interested in how a woman looks or dresses than in what kind of person she is. The Bible teaches a far different assessment of a woman's worth. It is the inner beauty of the godly woman that makes her so valuable.

Her character is displayed most vividly as she cares for her household. She is diligent and thrifty, providing for the needs of her husband and children. Such provision is the motivation for her work, whether it is in the home or on the job. Her speech also reveals her worth. Her communication with husband, children, and friends is encouraging and instructive. She realizes the importance of well-chosen words and their influence on her family.

She is vital to the success of the family. Her husband should be fully aware of that. He should also take time to understand her needs and meet them appropriately. She is to be treated as his spiritual equal. He is to love her in the same way that Christ loves the church—unconditionally, sacrificially, and wholeheartedly. So crucial is the relationship between a husband and his wife that his own prayers to God can be hindered if he treats her unfairly. Could anything shout her value to God more clearly?

Her children are to respect her and appreciate the many sacrifices she makes on their behalf. Their obedience to her is a demonstration of her importance and an acknowledgment of her spiritual wisdom.

A home, a community, a nation cannot function under God without the noble efforts of the godly woman. She is a unique

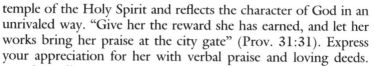

temple of the Holy Spirit and reflects the character of God in an unrivaled way. "Give her the reward she has earned, and let her works bring her praise at the city gate" (Prov. 31:31). Express your appreciation for her with verbal praise and loving deeds.

A godly woman is a treasure that should adorn every Christian home.

Father, thank you for making each of us so special. You have made woman to be cherished and treasured. Thank you for the example in the Scriptures of godly women who display your character.

TOUCHSTONE

A godly woman is a heavenly gift.

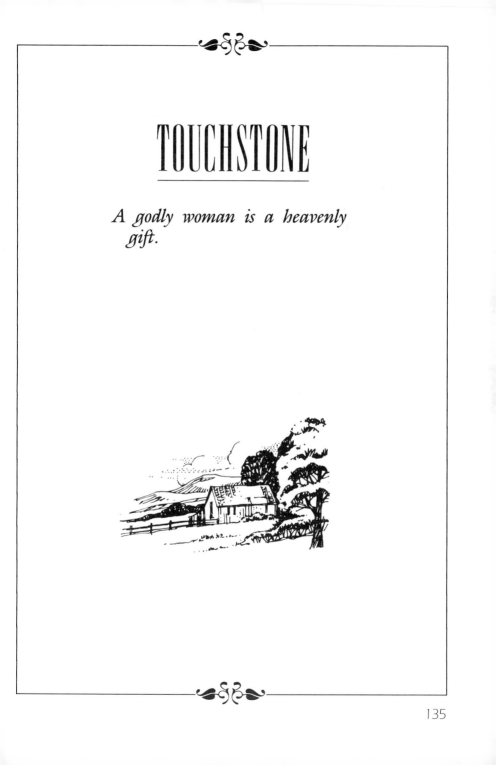